Guided Reading Strategies

HOLT

Civics in Practice

Principles of Government and Economics

HOLT, RINEHART AND WINSTON
A Harcourt Education Company
Orlando • Austin • New York • San Diego • London

Printed in the United States of America

ISBN 0-03-077988-X
20 19 18 17 16 15 12 11

Contents

Guided Reading Strategies

UNIT 1 A TRADITION OF DEMOCRACY

CHAPTER 1 We the People

1.1 Civics in Our Lives 1
1.2 Who Are U.S. Citizens? 2
1.3 The American People Today 3

CHAPTER 2 Foundations of Government

2.1 Why Americans Have Governments 4
2.2 The First Government 5
2.3 A New Constitution 6

CHAPTER 3 The U.S. Constitution

3.1 Ideals of the Constitution 7
3.2 The Three Branches of Government 8
3.3 An Enduring Document 9

CHAPTER 4 Rights and Responsibilities

4.1 The Bill of Rights 10
4.2 Guaranteeing Other Rights 11
4.3 Citizens' Duties and Responsibilities 12

UNIT 2 THE FEDERAL GOVERNMENT

CHAPTER 5 The Legislative Branch

5.1 The Senate and the House of Representatives 13
5.2 How Congress Is Organized 14
5.3 The Powers of Congress 15
5.4 How a Bill Becomes a Law 16

CHAPTER 6 The Executive Branch

6.1 The Presidency 17
6.2 Powers and Roles of the President 18
6.3 Executive Departments and the Cabinet 19
6.4 Independent Agencies and Regulatory Commissions 20

CHAPTER 7 The Judicial Branch

7.1 Equal Justice under the Law 21
7.2 The Federal Court System 22
7.3 The Supreme Court 23

UNIT 3 STATE AND LOCAL GOVERNMENT

CHAPTER 8 State Government

8.1 The States 24
8.2 State Legislatures 25
8.3 The State Executive Branch 26
8.4 State Courts 27

CHAPTER 9 Local Government

9.1 Units of Local Government 28
9.2 Town, Township, and Village Governments 29
9.3 City Government 30
9.4 How Governments Work Together 31

UNIT 4 THE CITIZEN IN GOVERNMENT

CHAPTER 10 Electing Leaders
10.1 A Two-Party System 32
10.2 Political Party Organization 33
10.3 The Right to Vote 34
10.4 Nominating and Electing Leaders 35

CHAPTER 11 The Political System
11.1 Shaping Public Opinion 36
11.2 Interest Groups 37
11.3 Taking Part in Government 38

CHAPTER 12 Paying for Government
12.1 Raising Money 39
12.2 Types of Taxes 40
12.3 Managing the Country's Money 41

UNIT 5 THE CITIZEN IN SOCIETY

CHAPTER 13 Citizenship and the Family
13.1 The Changing Family 42
13.2 Law and the Family 43
13.3 Your Family and You 44

CHAPTER 14 Citizenship in School
14.1 The U.S. School System 45
14.2 The Best Education for You 46
14.3 Developing Your Life Skills 47

CHAPTER 15 Citizenship in the Community
15.1 Kinds of Communities 48
15.2 Purposes of Communities 49
15.3 Citizens Serve Communities 50

CHAPTER 16 Citizenship and the Law
16.1 Crime in the United States 51
16.2 The Criminal Justice System 52
16.3 Juvenile Crime 53

UNIT 6 THE AMERICAN ECONOMY

CHAPTER 17 The Economic System
17.1 The Economic System at Work 54
17.2 Business Organizations 55
17.3 Making Business Decisions 56

CHAPTER 18 Goods and Services
18.1 American Production 57
18.2 Distributing Goods 58
18.3 You the Consumer 59

CHAPTER 19 Personal Finances
19.1 Money and Credit 60
19.2 Banks and Banking 61
19.3 Saving and Investing 62
19.4 Insurance against Hardship 63

CHAPTER 20 Economic Challenges
20.1 The Business Cycle 64
20.2 Coping with Economic Challenges 65
20.3 Labor and Management 66

CHAPTER 21 The U.S. Economy and the World
21.1 Overview of the US. Economy 67
21.2 Factors Affecting the U.S. Economy 68
21.3 Government's Role in the U.S. Economy 69
21.4 Living in a World Economy 70

CHAPTER 22 Career Choices
22.1 The Challenge of a Career 71
22.2 The World of Work 72
22.3 Unlimited Opportunities 73
22.4 Learning More about Careers 74
22.5 Learning More about Yourself 75

UNIT 7 THE UNITED STATES AND THE WORLD

CHAPTER 23 Foreign Policy
23.1 Conducting Foreign Relations 76
23.2 Working for Peace 77
23.3 The United Nations 78

CHAPTER 24 Charting a Course
24.1 Development of U.S. Foreign Policy 79
24.2 The Cold War 80
24.3 New Trends 81

Name ____________________ Class ____________ Date ____________

CHAPTER 1 Guided Reading Strategies 1.1

We the People

READING THE SECTION As you read this section, fill in the term that matches the following definitions or descriptions.

____________ **1.** The study of what it means to be a U.S. citizen

____________ **2.** Legally recognized member of a country

____________ **3.** Organizations, institutions, and individuals who exercise political authority over a group of people

____________ **4.** Ideas that people hold dear

____________ **5.** Values the U.S. government and American way of life are based on

____________ **6.** They govern through their elected officials.

POST-READING QUICK CHECK After reading the section, list the 10 characteristics of good citizens in the spaces below.

1. ____________________

2. ____________________

3. ____________________

4. ____________________

5. ____________________

6. ____________________

7. ____________________

8. ____________________

9. ____________________

10. ____________________

Name ______________________ Class ____________ Date ____________

CHAPTER 1 Guided Reading Strategies 1.2

We the People

READING THE SECTION As you read the section, match each term with the correct definition. Write the letter of the definition on the answer line.

_____ **1.** immigrant

_____ **2.** quota

_____ **3.** alien

_____ **4.** refugee

_____ **5.** native-born

_____ **6.** naturalization

a. number of immigrants that can come from a country or region

b. person born in any U.S. state or territory

c. person fleeing persecution in their homeland

d. person in the United States who is a citizen of another country

e. legal process by which an alien may become a citizen

f. person who comes to this country from other lands

POST-READING QUICK CHECK After reading the section, describe the naturalization process, or the steps by which an alien may become a U.S. citizen.

____

____

____

____

____

____

____

____

____

Name ______________________ Class ______________ Date ____________

CHAPTER 1 Guided Reading Strategies 1.3

We the People

READING THE SECTION As you read the section, complete each sentence below by writing the appropriate word or phrase in the space provided.

1. The main purpose of a(n) ______________________ is to find the size of each state's population.

2. The census provides information useful for studying ______________________.

3. People who live in the ______________________ now outnumber those living in cities.

4. Areas made up of cities and their suburbs are called ______________________.

5. Because of their warmer climates, states in the South and West, known as the ______________________, have experienced rapid population growth.

6. Population increases naturally when the ______________________ is higher than the ______________________.

7. In the 1800s farm workers and their families began a(n) ______________________ to cities.

8. The first U.S. census was in ______________________.

9. ______________________ million immigrants have come to the United States.

10. The U.S. population is getting ______________________ and more ______________________.

POST-READING QUICK CHECK After you have finished reading this section, list four states that lie in the Sunbelt.

1. ______________________ **3.** ______________________

2. ______________________ **4.** ______________________

Name ______________________ Class ______________ Date ____________

CHAPTER 2 Guided Reading Strategies 2.1

Foundations of Government

READING THE SECTION As you read the section, complete each sentence by writing the correct letter in the space provided.

_____ **1.** A government controlled by a king or queen is a
a. dictatorship.
b. monarchy.
c. totalitarian government.
d. democracy.

_____ **2.** A government in which one person holds all the power is a
a. dictatorship.
b. monarchy.
c. oligarchy
d. democracy.

_____ **3.** People rule directly or elect representatives who act on their behalf in this system of government.
a. dictatorship
b. monarchy
c. theocracy
d. democracy

_____ **4.** Voters in a community meet to make laws and decisions for their community in a
a. direct democracy.
b. representative democracy.
c. republic.
d. monarchy.

_____ **5.** People elect representatives to make laws for them in a
a. representative democracy.
b. dictatorship.
c. monarchy.
d. direct democracy.

_____ **6.** The rights and freedoms guaranteed to individuals are set out in
a. government services.
b. representative democracy.
c. the U.S. Constitution.
d. traditional beliefs.

_____ **7.** U.S. citizens are guaranteed the freedom of
a. laws.
b. education.
c. speech.
d. direct democracy.

POST-READING QUICK CHECK After you have finished reading the section, list five of the services that government provides to its citizens.

1. ____

2. ____

3. ____

4. ____

5. ____

Name ______________________ Class ______________ Date ____________

CHAPTER 2 Guided Reading Strategies 2.2

Foundations of Government

READING THE SECTION As you read the section, fill in the missing information in the space provided.

1. Colonial representatives who met in Philadelphia ______________________

2. Main author of the Declaration of Independence ______________________

3. Document that justifies separation from Great Britian and states American ideals

____

4. Basic rights to which all people are entitled ______________________

5. First U.S. plan of government, approved in 1781 ______________________

6. Loose association or league ______________________

7. State's absolute power or autonomy ______________________

POST-READING QUICK CHECK After you have finished reading the section, pretend you are a delegate to the meeting held in 1787 to revise the Articles of Confederation. Write six suggestions you would take to the meeting.

1. ______________________

____

2. ______________________

____

3. ______________________

____

4. ______________________

____

5. ______________________

____

6. ______________________

____

Name ______________________ Class ______________ Date ______________

CHAPTER 2 Guided Reading Strategies 2.3

Foundations of Government

READING THE SECTION As you read the section, match each of the terms in the left column with the correct definition from the right column in the space provided.

_____ **1.** Parliament

_____ **2.** federalism

_____ **3.** compromise

_____ **4.** ratification

_____ **5.** Federalists

_____ **6.** Antifederalists

a. sharing power between state and federal governments

b. approval

c. great Britain's lawmaking body

d. agreement made when opposing sides yield to reach a solution

e. opposed ratification of the Constitution

f. supporters of the Constitution

POST-READING QUICK CHECK After you have finished reading the section, fill in the term that fits the description in the space provided.

1. ______________________ document the Constitution replaced

2. ______________________ gathering of delegates to write and approve the Constitution

3. ______________________ city where the Constitutional Convention was held

4. ______________________ protected the rights of nobles against the British monarch in 1215

5. ______________________ included the right to petition and fair punishment for people found guilty of crimes in England

6. ______________________ kept an accurate journal of convention proceedings

7. ______________________ eighteenth-century movement that influenced the framers of the Constitution

8. ______________________ agreement to create a bicameral legislature called Congress

9. ______________________ series of articles that helped increase support for the Constitution

10. ______________________ became the first president of the United States in 1789

Name ______________________ Class ______________ Date ______________

CHAPTER 3 Guided Reading Strategies 3.1

The United States Constitution

READING THE SECTION As you read the section, complete the following chart by listing the powers that the Constitution provides under each column heading.

Federal Government	State Governments	Shared Powers

POST-READING QUICK CHECK After you read the section, consider whether the statements below are true or false. In the space provided write a *T* beside true statements and an *F* beside false statements.

_______ **1.** The Preamble explains why the Declaration of Independence was written.

_______ **2.** The Mayflower Compact established consent of the governed for the Pilgrims.

_______ **3.** In a federal system, there is only one level of government.

_______ **4.** The principle of majority rule in the United States disregards the rights of the minority.

_______ **5.** Limited government is government with defined restrictions on its power.

_______ **6.** Concurrent powers are powers left to the states.

_______ **7.** Rights guaranteed to the people of the United States are described in the Bill of Rights.

_______ **8.** State governments can raise funds through taxes, but the federal government cannot.

Name ______________________ Class ____________ Date ____________

CHAPTER 3 Guided Reading Strategies 3.2

The United States Constitution

READING THE SECTION As you read the section, fill in the missing information in the space provided.

1. Legislative branch

Main function (responsibility): **a.** ____________________

Two bodies: **b.** ____________________ and **c.** ____________________

A check it has over another branch of government: **d.** ____________________

2. Executive branch

Main function (responsibility): **e.** ____________________

Headed by (chief executive): **f.** ____________________

A check it has over another branch of government: **g.** ____________________

3. Judicial branch

Main function (responsibility): **h.** ____________________

Headed by: **i.** ____________________

A check it has over another branch of government: **j.** ____________________

POST-READING QUICK CHECK After you have finished reading the section, answer the following questions in the space provided.

1. Why was the system of checks and balances built into the Constitution?

____

2. Which branch has the power to create lower federal courts? ____________________

3. What is the difference between the terms *separation of powers* and *federalism?*

____

____

4. How may Congress override a presidential veto? ____________________

5. Which branch controls the allocation of funds? ____________________

Name ______________________ Class ______________ Date ____________

CHAPTER 3 Guided Reading Strategies 3.3

The United States Constitution

READING THE SECTION As you read the section, fill in the blanks to complete the following sentences.

1. The U.S. Constitution can be called an "______________________ document" because it can meet the changing conditions and needs of the country.

2. The Constitution can be adapted to meet changing needs in two ways: ______________________ and ______________________.

3. An ______________________ is a written change to the Constitution.

4. The section of the Constitution that outlines the process for changing the Constitution is ______________________.

5. Formal approval by the states of a change to the Constitution is known as ______________________.

6. If the people do not like the effects of an amendment, the amendment can be ______________________.

7. ______________________ sometimes interprets the Constitution in new ways to expand its authority to pass a certain law.

8. The ______________________ decides if new interpretations of the Constitution are legal.

9. The president's ______________________, or group of advisers, is an example of a change in the federal government that came about through custom and tradition.

10. Traditions of the federal government that are passed down through history are sometimes called the ______________________ Constitution.

POST-READING QUICK CHECK After reading the section, answer the following questions.

1. What are the two ways in which an amendment to the Constitution can be proposed?

2. What are the two ways in which an amendment may be ratified?

Name ______________________ Class ______________ Date ______________

CHAPTER 4 Guided Reading Strategies 4.1

Rights and Responsibilities

READING THE SECTION As you read the section, complete the following table by supplying the main rights protected by each amendment in the Bill of Rights.

Amendment	Main Rights
1. First	
2. Second	
3. Third	
4. Fourth	
5. Fifth	
6. Sixth	
7. Seventh	
8. Eighth	
9. Ninth	
10. Tenth	

POST-READING QUICK CHECK After you have finished reading the section, in the space provided, list three limits or exceptions to the rights listed in the Bill of Rights.

1. ______________________________

2. ______________________________

3. ______________________________

Name ______________________ Class ______________ Date ____________

CHAPTER 4 Guided Reading Strategies 4.2

Rights and Responsibilities

READING THE SECTION As you read the section, complete each sentence below by writing the appropriate term in the space provided.

1. Rights guaranteed to all U.S. citizens are called ____________________.

2. The ____________________ provides for due process and equal protection of the law for all Americans.

3. The ____________________ freed slaves throughout the United States and its territories.

4. The Fourteenth Amendment was added to the Constitution after the ____________________ to protect the rights of African Americans.

5. Voting rights were given to African Americans by the ____________________.

6. Direct election of senators by the people rather than through the state legislatures was established by the ____________________.

7. Women's ____________________ was granted by the Nineteenth Amendment.

8. The Twenty-third Amendment gave people living in Washington, D.C., the right to vote for ____________________.

9. The Twenty-fourth Amendment forbade the use of a(n) ____________________ as a voting qualification throughout the United States.

10. The ____________________ lowered the voting age in the United States from 21 to 18.

POST-READING QUICK CHECK After you have finished reading the section, name four of the women who were instrumental in winning voting rights for U.S. women.

1. ____

2. ____

3. ____

4. ____

Name ______________________ Class ____________ Date ____________

CHAPTER 4 Guided Reading Strategies 4.3

Rights and Responsibilities

READING THE SECTION As you read the section, complete each sentence by writing the correct letter in the space provided.

______ **1.** Ignorance of the law
- **a.** is important.
- **b.** is a good excuse.
- **c.** is no excuse.
- **d.** aids in driving.

______ **2.** Draft laws in the United States require
- **a.** all men and women over 18 to serve in the military.
- **b.** all men over 21 to serve in the military.
- **c.** all women over 18 to serve in the military.
- **d.** all men of certain ages and qualifications to serve in the military.

______ **3.** Citizens must, if called, report to serve as members of
- **a.** Congress.
- **b.** a jury.
- **c.** a local committee.
- **d.** a debate team.

______ **4.** By voting, each citizen is
- **a.** deciding who will lead the country.
- **b.** going to be ignored.
- **c.** placing his or her name on a mailing list.
- **d.** wasting time.

______ **5.** To cast their votes wisely, citizens should
- **a.** study law.
- **b.** be informed.
- **c.** watch TV.
- **d.** ask how their friends voted.

______ **6.** Americans must tell government representatives their
- **a.** opinions on public issues.
- **b.** financial problems.
- **c.** hopes and dreams.
- **d.** travel plans.

______ **7.** The quality of any government depends on the
- **a.** quality of people who serve.
- **b.** amount of taxes collected.
- **c.** quantity of political parties.
- **d.** president's political party.

______ **8.** Volunteering
- **a.** is not helpful.
- **b.** is an important way to help your community.
- **c.** will cause trouble.
- **d.** makes your neighbors angry

POST-READING QUICK CHECK After you have finished reading the section, list the five responsibilities of citizenship in the spaces provided, and write an example for each.

1. ____

2. ____

3. ____

4. ____

5. ____

Name ______________________ Class ______________ Date ____________

CHAPTER 5 Guided Reading Strategies 5.1

The Legislative Branch

READING THE SECTION As you read the section, answer the following questions in the spaces provided.

1. How many representatives are in the U.S. House of Representatives? ____________

2. How many senators are in the U.S. Senate? ____________

3. How are seats apportioned in the House of Representatives? How often does this process occur? ____________

____

4. Explain how gerrymandering affects congressional district boundaries. ____________

____

5. List the three qualifications for holding the office of U.S. representative. ____________

____

6. List the three qualifications for holding the office of U.S. senator. ____________

____

7. How many years does a U.S. representative serve in one term? ____________

8. How many years does a U.S. senator serve in one term? ____________

9. What percentage of senators are up for re-election at one time? ____________

POST-READING QUICK CHECK After you have finished reading the section, fill in the missing information in the space provided.

1. Give two examples of the codes of conduct Congress has passed for its members.

A. ____________

B. ____________

2. What is the difference between censure and the expulsion of a member of Congress?

____

____

Name ______________________ Class ______________ Date ______________

CHAPTER 5 Guided Reading Strategies 5.2

The Legislative Branch

READING THE SECTION As you read the section, match each of the following terms with the correct definitions in the space provided.

_____ **1.** sessions

_____ **2.** caucuses

_____ **3.** president *pro tempore*

_____ **4.** Speaker of the House

_____ **5.** whip

_____ **6.** joint session

_____ **7.** majority party

_____ **8.** minority party

_____ **9.** joint committees

_____ **10.** Twentieth amendment

a. political party that controls the House or Senate

b. assists floor leader by counting votes, encouraging party loyalty, and ensuring party members are present for important votes

c. private meetings of Congressional members by party

d. presides over the Senate in vice president's absence

e. handle housekeeping matters and do not have the authority to consider legislation

f. political party that has fewer members in the House or Senate

g. regular meetings of Congress

h. members of both houses of Congress meeting together

i. gives Congress the day and time when a term must begin every odd-numbered year

j. most powerful officer in the House of Representative

POST-READING QUICK CHECK After you have finished reading the section, answer the following questions in the space provided.

1. Who has the power to call a special session of Congress? ______________________

2. Who is customarily elected president *pro tempore?* ______________________

3. What are the titles of the two floor leaders for each house of Congress? ____________

4. What decides whether a political party will be the majority or minority party? ______

5. What position does the vice president of the United States hold in the Senate? ______

Name ______________________ Class ______________ Date ______________

CHAPTER 5 Guided Reading Strategies 5.3

The Legislative Branch

READING THE SECTION As you read the section, fill in the missing information in the spaces provided.

1. What is the elastic clause? ______________________

2. Why is treason an impeachable offense? ______________________

3. Which body of Congress has the power to impeach? ______________________

4. Where is the impeached official put on trial? ______________________

5. Under what circumstances would the vice president *not* preside over an impeachment trial? ______________________

6. Who presides over the impeachment trial when the vice president does not? ______________________

7. How many senators must vote for a conviction to remove an impeached official from office? ______________________

8. Name the two presidents who have been impeached. ______________________

POST-READING QUICK CHECK After you have finished reading the section, fill in the information about Congress in the spaces provided.

1. Name the three special powers delegated to the House of Representatives. ______________________

2. Name the four special powers delegated to the Senate. ______________________

3. Write an example of how a member of Congress may serve a constituent. ______________________

Name ______________________ Class ______________ Date ____________

CHAPTER 5 Guided Reading Strategies 5.4

The Legislative Branch

READING THE SECTION As you read the section, fill in the missing blanks with terms from the following list.

calendar	compromise bill	conference committee	reported out
president	simple majority	standing committee	subcommittee
two-thirds	veto		

Bill is introduced in the House or Senate. ➛ Bill is assigned identifying letters and numbers. ➛ Bill is referred to a Senate or House ______________. ➛ Bill is sent to ______________ for review. ➛ Hearings are held on bill; recommendations and changes are made. ➛ Committee votes and bill is ______________ of committee. ➛ Bill is placed on House or Senate ______________. ➛ Bill is debated on House or Senate floor. ➛ A ______________ is needed to pass the bill in the House or Senate. ➛ The bill now goes to the other body of Congress, and the process is repeated. ➛ If the bill passes in the other body of Congress, but the versions are not identical, the bill goes to a ______________ made up of members from both houses. ➛ A revised bill or ______________ then goes back to both houses and must pass in both bodies with a simple majority. ➛ If the bill passes in both houses, it then goes to the ______________, who may sign it into law. ➛ If instead the bill is rejected, then a ______________ has taken place. ➛ Congress may override a veto with a ______________ majority of both houses.

POST-READING QUICK CHECK After you have finished reading the section, answer the questions in the space provided.

1. Name five people or groups that can propose laws to Congress. ______________

____

2. Bills concerning money must originate in the ______________.

3. A debate on bills is generally limited to which body of Congress? ______________

4. A(n) ______________, or majority, must be present to do business.

5. Senators may try to keep a bill from coming up for a vote by making lengthy speeches known as ______________.

6. To limit debate, three fifths of the full Senate must vote for ______________.

Name ______________________ Class ______________ Date ______________

CHAPTER 6 Guided Reading Strategies 6.1

The Executive Branch

READING THE SECTION As you read the section, answer the following questions in the spaces provided.

1. What are the three qualifications for the office of president of the United States?

____

____

____

2. How many years does the president serve in one term? ______________

3. Which amendment limited the president to two terms? ______________

4. What is the annual salary for the president? ______________

5. What traits have all presidents shared so far? ______________

____

6. What jobs does the vice president officially have? ______________

____

7. How many vice presidents have taken over the office of president? ______________

POST-READING QUICK CHECK After reading the section, describe the changes the following amendments made to the Constitution.

1. Twentieth Amendment (1933) ______________

____

____

____

2. The Twenty-fifth Amendment (1967) ______________

____

____

____

Name ______________________ Class ____________ Date ____________

CHAPTER 6 Guided Reading Strategies 6.2

The Executive Branch

READING THE SECTION As you read the section, write in the duties the president performs in the following different roles.

1. Chief executive
1. ______________________
2. ______________________
3. ______________________
4. ______________________

2. Commander in chief
1. ______________________
2. ______________________

3. Foreign policy leader
1. ______________________
2. ______________________
3. ______________________

4. Judicial powers
1. ______________________
2. ______________________

POST-READING QUICK CHECK After reading the section, describe the following law in the space provided.

War Powers Resolution (1973) ______________________

____

____

____

Name ______________________ Class ______________ Date ______________

CHAPTER 6 Guided Reading Strategies 6.3

The Executive Branch

READING THE SECTION As you read the section, decide whether the following statements are true or false. Write a *T* in front of the true statements and an *F* in front of the false statements in the space provided.

______ **1.** The National Security Council advises in matters concerning the environment and water safety.

______ **2.** In 2005, there were 10 departments in the executive branch.

______ **3.** The head of the Department of Justice is the secretary of justice.

______ **4.** The secretary of state assists and advises the president in foreign affairs and foreign policy.

______ **5.** Visas allow U.S. citizens to travel to foreign countries.

______ **6.** Consuls represent the United States concerning commerce in foreign countries.

______ **7.** The Joint Chiefs of Staff include the highest-ranking officers of the armed forces.

______ **8.** It is the responsibility of the Department of Homeland Security to protect the nation against terrorist attacks.

______ **9.** The Department of the Treasury proposes the federal budget to Congress.

______ **10.** The Department of Justice provides federal assistance when natural disasters occur.

POST-READING QUICK CHECK After reading the section, write the word or words that would make the false statements above true. Write the number of the false statement with the correction(s).

____

____

____

____

____

CHAPTER 6 Guided Reading Strategies 6.4

The Executive Branch

READING THE SECTION As you read the section, write the job or duty of each of the following independent agencies or regulatory commissions in the space provided.

1. U.S. Commission on Civil Rights ______________________________

2. National Aeronautics and Space Administration ______________________________

3. Office of Personnel Management ______________________________

4. General Services Administration ______________________________

5. Federal Election Commission ______________________________

6. Consumer Product Safety Commission ______________________________

7. Securities and Exchange Commission ______________________________

8. National Labor Relations Board ______________________________

POST-READING QUICK CHECK After reading the section, fill in the blanks with the correct answers to complete each statement.

1. The more than 65 independent agencies that ____________________ created assist the president in carrying out his duties.

2. Independent agencies that bring violators to court are called

____________________.

3. The ____________________ appoints the heads of the regulatory commissions.

4. Appointments to the regulatory commissions must be approved by the

____________________.

5. About 3 million people work in the federal ____________________, which performs the day-to-day work of the executive branch.

Name ______________________ Class ______________ Date ____________

CHAPTER 7 Guided Reading Strategies 7.1

The Judicial Branch

READING THE SECTION As you read the section, match each of the following terms with the correct definition in the space provided.

_____ **1.** crime

_____ **2.** criminal law

_____ **3.** civil law

_____ **4.** the Constitution

_____ **5.** statutory laws

_____ **6.** majority rule

_____ **7.** common law

_____ **8.** precedent

_____ **9.** administrative law

_____ **10.** constitutional law

_____ **11.** Sixth Amendment

_____ **12.** appeal

a. law based on the Constitution and on Supreme Court decisions interpreting the Constitution

b. any behavior that is considered illegal

c. laws created by government agencies

d. an earlier court decision

e. group of laws that defines what acts are crimes

f. what the majority of citizens believe to be right or wrong

g. group of laws that refers to disputes between people

h. process by which a convicted person asks a higher court to review the result of a trial

i. guarantees that a defendant in a criminal case has the right to the "assistance of counsel"

j. laws passed by lawmaking bodies

k. law that comes from judges' decisions

l. the supreme law of the land

POST-READING QUICK CHECK After reading the section, write the correct answers in the spaces provided.

List the sources of law in the United States.

1. ____

2. ____

3. ____

4. ____

Name ______________________ Class ____________ Date ____________

CHAPTER 7 Guided Reading Strategies 7.2

The Judicial Branch

READING THE SECTION After reading the section, fill in the blanks with the correct answer to complete each statement.

1. District courts have original ____________________, or the authority to hear cases for the first time.

2. Courts of appeals have ____________________ jurisdiction.

3. The federal court system is divided into ____________________ district courts and ____________________ judicial circuits.

4. In a court of appeals, a ____________________ of judges makes decisions on cases.

5. The court of appeals may send a case back to the district court for a new trial, or it may ____________________ the decision.

6. Federal judges are appointed to serve ____________________ terms.

7. Federal judges are appointed by the ____________________ and must be confirmed by the ____________________.

8. The decisions of the Supreme Court justices cannot be ____________________.

POST-READING QUICK CHECK After reading the section, write the appropriate answer(s) in the space provided.

1. What are the two types of jurisdiction? ____________________

____

2. What is the job or function of courts of appeals? ____________________

3. Name the three types of cases that go before the Supreme Court. ____________________

____

Name ______________________ Class ______________ Date ______________

CHAPTER 7 Guided Reading Strategies 7.3

The Judicial Branch

READING THE SECTION As you read the section, complete each sentence by writing the correct letter in the space provided.

_____ **1.** The power of judicial review allows courts to
a. decide if a judge must be impeached.
b. reject cases.
c. decide whether a law or presidential action is unconstitutional.
d. send cases to Congress for review.

_____ **2.** The return of a case to a lower court for a new trial is called a
a. remand.
b. docket.
c. brief.
d. check.

_____ **3.** When a justice agrees with the majority decision but for differing reasons, he or she might write a(n)
a. opinion.
b. concurring opinion.
c. dissenting opinion.
d. demand.

_____ **4.** The justice who disagrees with the majority might write a(n)
a. opinion to serve.
b. concurring opinion.
c. dissenting opinion.
d. demand.

_____ **5.** The case that established the "reading of rights" to a suspect was
a. *Miranda* v. *Arizona.*
b. *Brown* v. *Board of Education.*
c. *Plessy* v. *Ferguson.*
d. *Marbury* v. *Madison.*

_____ **6.** The case that established the "separate but equal rights" was
a. *Miranda* v. *Arizona.*
b. *Brown* v. *Board of Education.*
c. *Plessy* v. *Ferguson.*
d. *Marbury* v. *Madison.*

POST-READING QUICK CHECK After you have finished reading the section, write the answers in the spaces provided.

1. What can Congress do if the Supreme Court declares a law unconstitutional?

____

____

2. Who determines the size of the Supreme Court? What number has it been set at since 1869?

____

Name ______________________ Class ______________ Date ______________

CHAPTER 8 Guided Reading Strategies 8.1

State Government

READING THE SECTION As you read the section, list the information in the spaces provided for the reserved and concurrent powers.

State powers (reserved)

1. ______________________________

2. ______________________________

3. ______________________________

4. ______________________________

5. ______________________________

Shared powers (concurrent)

6. ______________________________

7. ______________________________

8. ______________________________

9. ______________________________

POST-READING QUICK CHECK After reading the section, fill in the blanks with the correct answers to complete each statement.

1. The ______________________ protects the rights of state governments.

2. Taxation is an example of a(n) ______________________ power.

3. The ______________________ ensures that states accept the decisions of courts in other states.

4. Returning fugitives to other states is known as ______________________.

5. Some of the items that most state constitutions contain are ______________________

____

____.

Name ______________________ Class ______________ Date ______________

CHAPTER 8 Guided Reading Strategies 8.2

State Government

READING THE SECTION As you read the section, match each of the following terms with the correct definition in the space provided.

_____ **1.** bicameral

_____ **2.** unicameral

_____ **3.** constituent

_____ **4.** initiative

_____ **5.** referendum

_____ **6.** recall

a. one-house legislature

b. citizens represented by lawmakers

c. process that allows citizens to start new legislation

d. two-house legislature

e. method of referring potential laws directly to the people

f. an election held to remove an elected official from office

POST-READING QUICK CHECK After reading the section, answer the following questions in the spaces provided.

1. Which state has the only unicameral legislature? ______________________

2. What court case in 1964 established that all state election districts be equal?

____

3. Which state has the smallest legislature, with only 40 representatives and 20 senators?

____

4. Which state only pays state legislators $10,000 annually? ______________________

5. Which state pays state legislators $79,500 annually? ______________________

6. What state legislature meets the entire period for a two-year session? ____________

____

7. If a bill passes in both houses but not in identical forms, what would be the next step in the lawmaking process? ______________________

CHAPTER 8 Guided Reading Strategies 8.3

State Government

READING THE SECTION As you read the section, write an example for each of the following duties that governors perform.

chief legislator **1.** ______________________

chief executive **2.** ______________________

political party leader **3.** ______________________

other **4.** ______________________

POST-READING QUICK CHECK After reading the section, fill in the blanks with the appropriate answer concerning the executive branch.

1. If the governor dies or is removed from office, the ______________________ would be next in line to become governor.

2. The executive official in charge of keeping state records and carrying out election laws is the ______________________.

3. The ______________________ handles state legal matters.

4. Handling state funds is the job of the ______________________.

5. The ______________________ examines state financial records and payments.

6. The state auditor is sometimes called the ______________________.

7. Carrying out policies of the state board of education is performed by the ______________________, who also handles the distribution of state funds to local districts.

8. Some state jobs are filled by people recommended by political party leaders through a practice known as ______________________.

Name ____________________ Class ____________ Date ____________

CHAPTER 8 Guided Reading Strategies 8.4

State Government

READING THE SECTION As you read the section, match each of the following terms with the correct definitions in the space provided.

______ **1.** penal code	**a.** set of criminal laws
______ **2.** criminal case	**b.** deals with violations of the law
______ **3.** civil case	**c.** method of selecting judges
______ **4.** trial court	**d.** deals with disputes between individuals and businesses
______ **5.** municipal court	**e.** court that is divided to hear specific types of cases
______ **6.** small claims court	**f.** hears civil cases involving small sums of money
______ **7.** appeal	**g.** request for another court to consider case
______ **8.** Missouri Plan	**h.** handles major criminal and civil cases

POST-READING QUICK CHECK After reading the section, write the correct answers in the spaces provided.

1. How do courts of appeals cases differ from general trial court cases?

____

____

____

Name the two ways state supreme court judges are selected.

2. ____

3. ____

CHAPTER 9 Guided Reading Strategies 9.1

Local Government

READING THE SECTION As you read the section, name the term or office that each of the following statements describes.

1. Local government incorporated by the state ______________

2. The largest type of municipality______________

3. Division of state government formed to carry out state laws, collect taxes, and supervise elections ______________

4. Head law enforcement official for counties ______________

5. Basic plan for local government that defines its powers, responsibilities, and organization ______________

6. Regulations that govern the community ______________

POST-READING QUICK CHECK After you have finished reading the section, list the answers in the spaces provided.

1. List at least six services that local governments provide for citizens. ______________

2. Who are some county officials and what are their jobs? ______________

3. Why is it important for local and state governments to work together? Be sure to include specific examples.

Name ______________________ Class ____________ Date ____________

CHAPTER 9 Guided Reading Strategies 9.2

Local Government

READING THE SECTION As you read the section, match each of the following terms with the correct definitions in the space provided.

_______ **1.** Law enforcement official for a township

_______ **2.** Form of local government that started in the New England colonies and included homes, churches, and outlying farms

_______ **3.** Units of local government created in the Midwest in areas divided by Congress

_______ **4.** Public meeting where residents can discuss and vote on issues

_______ **5.** Unit of government formed to meet a special need for a specific area

_______ **6.** Small unit of local government used in colonial New York, New Jersey, and Pennsylvania

_______ **7.** Self-governing municipality in a rural community with at least 200 to 300 residents

_______ **8.** The executive of the small council in a village or borough who is elected by voters

a. town
b. village
c. constable
d. town meeting
e. special district
f. township
g. civil townships
h. mayor

POST-READING QUICK CHECK After you have finished reading the section, answer the following questions in the spaces provided.

1. What is the governing body of local school districts called? What is the executive called?

____

____

2. How can residents organize their local community into a village or borough form of government? ______________________________

____

____

Name ______________________ Class ______________ Date ____________

CHAPTER 9 Guided Reading Strategies 9.3

Local Government

READING THE SECTION As you read the section, fill in the missing information to complete the following chart.

Three Forms of City Government	Main Points of Each Form
mayor-council	1. 2. 3.
commission	1. 2. 3.
council-manager	1. 2. 3.

POST-READING QUICK CHECK After you have finished reading the section, answer the following questions in the spaces provided.

1. How is home rule different from traditional city government?

____

2. Which of the three types of city government is the oldest and most commonly used?

____

3. Where was the commission form of city government introduced?

____

4. How is the city manager chosen in a council-manager form of government?

____

Name ______________________ Class ______________ Date ______________

CHAPTER 9 Guided Reading Strategies 9.4

Local Government

READING THE SECTION As you read the section, complete each sentence by writing the correct letter in the space provided.

______ **1.** All levels of government must
- **a.** control public schools.
- **b.** obey the U.S. Constitution.
- **c.** give grants-in-aid.
- **d.** have charters.

______ **2.** In colonial days, building a road was
- **a.** a local project.
- **b.** the state's responsibility.
- **c.** the job of the U.S. government.
- **d.** an example of cooperation between governments.

______ **3.** In 1893, Massachusetts established
- **a.** block grants.
- **b.** interstate highways.
- **c.** public schools.
- **d.** a state highway commission.

______ **4.** President Eisenhower was instrumental in the development of the
- **a.** state highway departments.
- **b.** U.S. Coast Guard.
- **c.** U.S. federal government.
- **d.** interstate highway system.

______ **5.** Control of schools is left to
- **a.** the federal government.
- **b.** state boards of education.
- **c.** local boards of education.
- **d.** the U.S. Conference of Mayors.

______ **6.** Block grants are given
- **a.** for specific projects.
- **b.** to the federal government.
- **c.** for broadly defined purposes.
- **d.** all of the above

______ **7.** To make sure professional workers are qualified, states establish
- **a.** licensing boards.
- **b.** boards of education.
- **c.** health regulations.
- **d.** bank inspectors.

______ **8.** States compete with each other to attract
- **a.** tax breaks.
- **b.** licensing boards.
- **c.** industry.
- **d.** cooperation.

POST-READING QUICK CHECK After reading the section, list at least three ways governments cooperate.

1. ____

2. ____

3. ____

Name ______________________ Class ______________ Date ______________

CHAPTER 10 Guided Reading Strategies 10.1

Electing Leaders

READING THE SECTION Read the following statements and write a *T* in front of the true statements and an *F* in front of the false statements. If false, explain why.

______ **1.** Political parties are made up of citizens with similar views on public issues.

____

______ **2.** Political parties nominate the individuals who run for election to public office.

____

______ **3.** The United States has a multiparty system. ______________________

____

______ **4.** The Democratic Party is said to be more conservative.

____

______ **5.** The multiparty systems found in several European countries have the advantage of easily forming stable governments. ______________________

______ **6.** Coalition governments are common to the multiparty system.

____

______ **7.** One-party systems are examples of dictatorships and totalitarian governments.

____

______ **8.** In 1912 Theodore Roosevelt formed the Populist party. ______________

______ **9.** Ross Perot's involvement in the 1992 election may have cost Bill Clinton the election. ______________________

______**10.** Third-party views and platforms often are adopted by mainstream parties.

____

POST-READING QUICK CHECK After you have finished reading the section, write the advantages of the two-party system over one-party or multiparty systems.

____

____

CHAPTER 10 Guided Reading Strategies 10.2

Electing Leaders

READING THE SECTION As you read the section, fill in the correct information about the different types of committees in the spaces provided on the chart.

COMMITTEES	METHODS OF MEMBER AND/OR CHAIRPERSON SELECTION	DUTIES AND RESPONSIBILITIES
Local Committees		
State Committees		
National Committees		

POST-READING QUICK CHECK After you have finished reading the section, answer the following questions concerning political parties and campaigns.

1. How did the Federal Election Campaign Act reform campaign contributions? What agency monitors contributions? ____________________

____

____

____

2. What are the eligibility requirements for candidates to obtain matching public funds in federal elections? ____________________

____

____

____

____

Name ______________________ Class ____________ Date ____________

CHAPTER 10 Guided Reading Strategies 10.3

Electing Leaders

READING THE SECTION As you read the section, match the following terms with the appropriate definition by writing the correct letter in the space provided.

_____ **1.** independent voters	**a.** first election to choose party candidates to run in a later election
_____ **2.** primary election	**b.** election in which voters may vote for candidates of either party
_____ **3.** general election	**c.** ballots marked in privacy
_____ **4.** closed primary	**d.** election in which voters choose their leaders
_____ **5.** open primary	**e.** voters who are not members of a political party
_____ **6.** secret ballot	**f.** election in which only registered party members can vote to choose the party's candidates

POST-READING QUICK CHECK After you have finished reading the section, write the answers to the questions in the spaces provided.

1. How does voter registration protect a citizen's vote? ______________________

____

2. How are independent candidates placed on the general ballot in an election?

____

____

3. What voting methods are used today? ______________________

____

____

CHAPTER 10 Guided Reading Strategies 10.4

Electing Leaders

READING THE SECTION As you read the section, fill in the following outline concerning the electoral college in the spaces provided.

I. ELECTORAL COLLEGE

A. Voters Elect Electors

1. Your vote for president is actually cast for people called ____________________.

2. An elector is ____.

3. There are _____ electors in the electoral college.

4. If the Democratic candidate wins the ____________ vote in a state, then the Democratic ________ cast that state's electoral votes.

B. Electors Elect the President

5. A few weeks after election day, electors ____________________________________.

6. The candidate who receives _________________________ becomes the next president.

7. The ________________________ chooses the president if no candidate receives a majority of electoral votes.

8. Neither presidential candidate received a majority of votes in _____ elections in U.S. history.

POST-READING QUICK CHECK After you have finished reading the section, answer the following question on the nomination process in the space provided.

Explain what happens at a party convention.

____

____

____

CHAPTER 11 Guided Reading Strategies 11.1

The Political System

READING THE SECTION As you read the section, complete each sentence below by writing the appropriate term in the space provided.

1. The total of the opinions held concerning a particular issue is called

______________________.

2. ______________________ includes television, radio, newspapers, books, films, and magazines.

3. Ideas that are spread to influence people are called ______________________.

4. ______________________ is used to fool people without letting them know that its purpose is to influence their views.

5. ______________________ makes readers or listeners aware that someone is trying to influence them.

6. Endorsements from famous individuals such as professional athletes are considered

______________________, one type of propaganda technique.

7. The ______________________ technique is a type of propaganda that appeals to people's desire to do what their friends and neighbors are doing.

8. The use of negative or unpleasant descriptions or labels is often used in campaigns

and is known as ______________________.

9. Using facts or statistics in a manner that favors a particular product, idea, or candi-

date is called ______________________.

10. A ______________________ attempts to measure public opinion by asking the opinions of a sample of the public.

POST-READING QUICK CHECK What are six types of propaganda techniques?

____

____

____

CHAPTER 11 Guided Reading Strategies 11.2

The Political System

READING THE SECTION As you read the section, fill in the blanks with the correct information in the space provided.

1. Organizations of people with a common interest that try to influence government policies ____________________
2. Another name for an interest or pressure group ____________________
3. A person who is paid by an interest group to represent that group's interest ____________________
4. Groups that promote the interests of the general public ____________________ ____________________
5. Act that tightened lobbying regulations by closing many loopholes ____________________ ____________________ ____________________

POST-READING QUICK CHECK After you have finished reading the section, answer the following questions in the spaces provided.

1. What are some of the methods that lobbyists use to influence or help lawmakers?

____

____

2. Describe how the government keeps records of interest groups.

____

____

CHAPTER 11 Guided Reading Strategies 11.3

The Political System

READING THE SECTION As you read the section, write the correct information or examples concerning government participation in the spaces provided.

1. List four ways that individuals may participate in government.

a. ______________________________

b. ______________________________

c. ______________________________

d. ______________________________

2. List five reasons why the voter turnout rate is lower in the United States than in most other democratic nations.

a. ______________________________

b. ______________________________

c. ______________________________

d. ______________________________

e. ______________________________

POST-READING QUICK CHECK After reading the section, answer the following questions in the spaces provided.

1. How do political action committees (PACs) contribute money to individual candidates in an election?

____

____

2. How can individuals express their opinions on issues to local officials and congressmembers?

____

____

Name ______________________ Class ______________ Date ______________

CHAPTER 12 Guided Reading Strategies 12.1

Paying for Government

READING THE SECTION As you read the section, decide which of the following statements are true and which are false. Write a *T* in front of the true statements and write a *F* in front of the false statements in the spaces provided. If false, explain why.

______ **1.** One of the largest expenditures of the federal government is national defense.

____

______ **2.** The main source of government revenue is the national debt.

____

______ **3.** Taxes are set at different rates for different age groups.

____

______ **4.** Equal application of taxes would make sales taxes the same rate for similar items. ____

______ **5.** Scheduled payments of taxes would include withholdings from workers' paychecks. ____

______ **6.** Fees are sources of revenue from people who break certain laws, such as those regarding traffic. ____

______ **7.** The fees charged for drivers licenses and automobile licenses are a major source of revenue for state governments. ____

______ **8.** Government borrowing from individuals would be an example of a fine.

____

______ **9.** Bonds include a promise to repay the amount borrowed, with interest, on the maturity date. ____

POST-READING QUICK CHECK After you have finished reading the section, list the three main ways that federal, state, and local governments raise funds.

____

____

Name ______________________ Class ______________ Date ____________

CHAPTER 12 Guided Reading Strategies 12.2

Paying for Government

READING THE SECTION As you read the section, complete each sentence by writing the correct letter in the space provided.

______ **1.** The largest source of federal government revenue is the
a. property tax.
b. income tax.
c. excise tax.
d. estate tax.

______ **2.** The individual income tax is an example of a
a. progressive tax.
b. regressive tax.
c. tariff.
d. none of the above

______ **3.** Corporate income taxes are based on a corporation's
a. Social Security payments.
b. revenues.
c. expenses.
d. profits.

______ **4.** A sales tax is an example of a
a. progressive tax.
b. regressive tax.
c. tariff.
d. none of the above

______ **5.** Excise taxes are collected on
a. luxury items.
b. most products sold.
c. all imported products.
d. all property.

______ **6.** Property taxes are collected on
a. real property.
b. personal property.
c. both a and b.
d. none of the above

______ **7.** Gift taxes must be paid on gifts worth more than
a. $1,100.
b. $11 million.
c. $11.
d. $11,000.

______ **8.** Today the United States uses tariffs mainly to
a. raise money.
b. hurt American consumers.
c. regulate foreign trade.
d. fund Social Security payments.

POST-READING QUICK CHECK After reading the section, list the different kinds of taxes collected by the levels of U.S. government.

____

____

____

Name ______________________ Class ______________ Date ____________

CHAPTER 12 Guided Reading Strategies 12.3

Paying for Government

READING THE SECTION Read through the following descriptions. As you read the section provide the correct term for each description in the space provided.

1. ______________________ Agency of the Treasury Department that handles the federal collection of taxes

2. ______________________ Federal agency in charge of collecting tariffs on imported goods

3. ______________________ State or local official responsible for ensuring public funds are spent as authorized

4. ______________________ Federal official responsible for planning the federal budget

5. ______________________ Federal agency that helps prepare the federal budget

6. ______________________ Federal body that must turn the federal budget into law

7. ______________________ When government revenue equals government expenditures

8. ______________________ When government collects more than it spends

9. ______________________ When government spends more than it collects

10. ______________________ An accountant's examination of every item of income and expenditure

POST-READING QUICK CHECK After you have read the section, explain in the space provided how the legislative branch finalizes the federal budget and authorizes the spending of funds.

____

____

____

CHAPTER 13 Guided Reading Strategies 13.1

Citizenship and the Family

READING THE SECTION As you read the section, complete each sentence by writing the correct letter in the space provided.

______ **1.** The percentage of Americans who live in rural areas today is
- **a.** 50 percent.
- **b.** 16 percent.
- **c.** 10 percent.
- **d.** 21 percent.

______ **2.** Many Americans moved to urban areas because of
- **a.** new inventions.
- **b.** the rise of factories.
- **c.** improved methods of production.
- **d.** all of the above

______ **3.** The average age for women to marry in 2000 was
- **a.** 20.3.
- **b.** 22.8.
- **c.** 25.1.
- **d.** 26.7.

______ **4.** Which of the following is a reason for delayed marriages?
- **a.** economic necessity
- **b.** growing acceptance of singlehood
- **c.** finishing education and starting a career
- **d.** all of the above

______ **5.** More than ____________ of marriages taking place today are remarriages.
- **a.** 20 percent
- **b.** 30 percent
- **c.** 40 percent
- **d.** 50 percent

______ **6.** About __________ percent of American families with children under 18 live in single-parent families.
- **a.** 27
- **b.** 25
- **c.** 50
- **d.** 62

POST-READING QUICK CHECK After you have finished reading the section, list some of the marriage trends taking place in the United States today.

____

____

____

____

____

____

____

Name ______________________ Class ______________ Date ____________

CHAPTER 13 Guided Reading Strategies 13.2

Citizenship and the Family

READING THE SECTION As you read the section, fill in the blanks with the correct word or phrase in the space provided.

1. Laws that govern family life, including marriage and divorce, are passed by the

______________________.

2. In most states, people under the age of 18 are required by law to have

______________________ before they can marry.

3. Waiting periods and a(n) ______________________ are required in some states before a couple can obtain a marriage license.

4. Doctors and teachers must report suspected cases of ______________________ to the proper authorities.

5. Children who have been abused may be placed in ______________________ to be cared for properly.

6. A person who is appointed by the state court to care for a minor would be the

minor's ______________________.

7. To ______________________ a child is to legally establish him or her as a member of a family.

8. In a(n) ______________________, couples do not have to charge their partners with grounds, just irreconcilable differences.

9. Division of property, ______________________ of children, and child support are some of the issues and decisions that divorcing couples must face.

10. One possible reason for the high divorce rate in the United States is that the

______________________ has become less complicated.

POST-READING QUICK CHECK After you have finished reading the section, list some state marriage laws.

____

____

____

CHAPTER 13 Guided Reading Strategies 13.3

Citizenship and the Family

READING THE SECTION As you read the section, complete the following chart by filling in the correct information concerning families and their chief functions in American society.

Five Functions Of Families	Description/Example of Each Function
1.	**A.**
2.	**B.**
3.	**C.**
4.	**D.**
5.	**E.**

POST-READING QUICK CHECK After you have finished reading the section, list some ways in the space provided that you could be more (1) respectful of, (2) helpful to, and (3) considerate of family members.

1. ____

____

2. ____

____

3. ____

____

Name ______________________ Class ______________ Date ____________

CHAPTER 14 Guided Reading Strategies 14.1

Citizenship in School

READING THE SECTION As you read the section, complete the following statements by filling in the blanks.

1. Education helps ______________________ grow.

2. Education builds a strong ______________________.

3. Children three and four years old may attend ______________________ to learn how to play and get along with other children.

4. ______________________ is where children learn the building blocks of reading, writing, and mathematics.

5. High schools that provide a college preparatory curriculum are known as

______________________ high schools.

6. Technical and ______________________ high schools provide occupational training.

7. Two-year ______________________ are often supported by tax money and provide specialized job training and prep courses for transferring to a four-year college.

8. A(n) ______________________ is made up of one or more colleges.

9. Students with special needs are often taught in regular classrooms when possible, a

practice known as ______________________.

10. ______________________ are ideas that people hold dear and try to live by.

POST-READING QUICK CHECK After you have finished reading the section, answer the following questions in the spaces provided.

1. What are the seven traditional values found in the American educational process?

____

2. What are some of the challenges facing the American public school system? What are some possible solutions to these problems?

____

Name ______________________ Class ______________ Date ____________

CHAPTER 14 Guided Reading Strategies 14.2

Citizenship in School

READING THE SECTION As you read the section, write each of the seven goals of schools in the space beside the correct definition.

1. Teaching reading, writing, etc. ______________________

2. Teaching how to cooperate with others ______________________

3. Teaching good hygiene, fitness, etc. ______________________

4. Specialized career training, preparing for future ______________________

5. Teaching democratic principles ______________________

6. Teaching respectful attitudes ______________________

7. Teaching hobbies and enrichment ______________________

POST-READING QUICK CHECK After you have finished reading the section, fill in the information asked for in the spaces provided.

1. Write at least five of the study habits and textbook hints that can help you become a better organized student.

____

2. List at least four of the values and skills that extracurricular activities can provide to help students later in life.

____

Name ______________________ Class ______________ Date ____________

CHAPTER 14 Guided Reading Strategies 14.3

Citizenship in School

READING THE SECTION As you read the section, match each of the following terms with the correct definition by placing the correct letter in the space provided.

_____ **1.** experience

_____ **2.** conditioning

_____ **3.** habit

_____ **4.** motivation

_____ **5.** insight

_____ **6.** creativity

_____ **7.** critical thinking

_____ **8.** prejudice

a. action that is performed automatically without thinking about it

b. observation of or participation in events

c. thinking that comes from your heart more than your mind

d. opinion that is not based on careful and reasonable investigation of the facts

e. learning that takes place when behaviors are punished or rewarded

f. ability to find new ways of thinking and doing things

g. type of reasoning that involves a number of steps to reach decisions and solve problems

h. internal drive to achieve your goals

POST-READING QUICK CHECK After you have finished reading the section, think of a current problem at home or school and then use the critical-thinking steps to come up with a possible solution. List each step before writing the applicable information for your particular problem.

Name ______________________ Class ______________ Date ____________

CHAPTER 15 Guided Reading Strategies 15.1

Citizenship in the Community

READING THE SECTION As you read the section, complete the following sentences by filling in the blanks.

1. A(n) ______________________ is a group of people who have common interests and live in the same area.

2. ______________________ are natural features of land that people use for living.

3. Good weather, or ______________________, tends to attract settlers to an area.

4. Mineral resources such as coal, iron, and petroleum helped fuel the ________________.

5. Successful farming depends on having a long enough ______________________.

6. Some of the largest American cities, such as Boston, New York, Philadelphia, and ______________________, began as seaports.

7. Port towns along the Mississippi River, such as ______________________ and ______________________, grew into major cities.

8. Communities often spring up at places where two main roads meet, called ______________________.

9. When ______________________ began spreading across the country in the late 1840s, they created new settlements.

10. A(n) ______________________ is a region of farms and small towns.

11. According to the 2000 census, 80 percent of all Americans live in ________________.

12. A(n) ______________________ is a town, village, or community located on the outskirts of a city.

POST-READING QUICK CHECK After you have finished reading the section, think of some other U.S. cities (other than those mentioned in the section) that are located at crossroads. List five cities and the transportation routes that they are near.

____

____

Name ______________________ Class ______________ Date ____________

CHAPTER 15 Guided Reading Strategies 15.2

Citizenship in the Community

READING THE SECTION As you read the section, fill in the blanks in the following outline on the resons people live in communities..

1. **Communication:** List the two basic values of communities.

   a. ______________ **b.** ______________

2. **Recreation:** Relaxation or amusement by playing or doing something different from one's usual activities. List eight types of recreation.

   a. ______________ **b.** ______________ **c.** ______________

   d. ______________ **e.** ______________ **f.** ______________

   g. ______________ **h.** ______________

3. **Local government:** Provides laws and regulations needed to keep order. List three groups that maintain peace and order.

   a. ______________ **b.** ______________ **c.** ______________

4. **Community services:** Provide better services to meet certain citizen needs. List six types of community services.

   a. ______________ **b.** ______________ **c.** ______________

   d. ______________ **e.** ______________ **f.** ______________

POST-READING QUICK CHECK After reading the section, list four examples of community recreational facilities.

1. ____

2. ____

3. ____

4. ____

CHAPTER 15 Guided Reading Strategies 15.3

Citizenship in the Community

READING THE SECTION As you read the section, write the correct term or phrase to fill in the blanks and complete each statement.

1. Some citizenship services are required by law, which means they are

________________________.

2. Two examples of compulsory laws are ________________________ and

________________________.

3. ________________________ work to improve the community.

4. A small volunteer group may be formed for a specific ________________________, such as cleaning up the neighborhood.

5. Throughout your life you have ________________________ to be an active citizen.

6. What you decide about your level of community ________________________ will be influenced by your interests, your values, your age, and other things going on in your life.

7. Volunteer groups are supported by money from private ________________________, but they depend on the work of local volunteers.

8. You can support volunteer groups with your ________________________,

________________________, or ________________________.

POST-READING QUICK CHECK After reading the section, write down examples of how you can be a good citizen.

____

____

____

____

____

Name ______________________ Class ______________ Date ____________

CHAPTER 16 Guided Reading Strategies 16.1

Citizenship and the Law

READING THE SECTION As you read the section, match each of the following terms with the correct definition in the space provided.

_____ **1.** crime
_____ **2.** criminal
_____ **3.** felonies
_____ **4.** misdemeanors
_____ **5.** homicide
_____ **6.** aggravated assault
_____ **7.** forcible rape
_____ **8.** burglary
_____ **9.** larceny
_____ **10.** motor vehicle theft
_____ **11.** robbery
_____ **12.** vandalism
_____ **13.** arson
_____ **14.** victimless crimes
_____ **15.** embezzlement
_____ **16.** fraud
_____ **17.** white-collar crimes
_____ **18.** organized crime

a. killing of one person by another person
b. act that breaks the law
c. physical injury done intentionally to another
d. serious crimes like homicide
e. forcible and illegal entry with intention to steal
f. the willful destruction of property
g. destruction of property by setting fire to it
h. nonviolent crimes such as copyright infringement and fraud
i. less serious offenses like traffic violations
j. theft of money entrusted to an individual's care
k. theft of property without use of force or violence
l. taking someone else's money or property dishonestly
m. groups specializing in providing illegal goods and services
n. crime that involves both property and persons
o. person who commits any type of crime
p. when a criminal does not violate another person's rights
q. theft of automobiles
r. sexual violation of a person by force and against the person's will

POST-READING QUICK CHECK After you read the section, list three reasons why the crime rate is so high in the United States. Also list three ways to prevent crime.

____

____

____

CHAPTER 16 Guided Reading Strategies 16.2

Citizenship and the Law

READING THE SECTION As you read the section, complete each sentence by writing the letter of the correct term in the space provided.

______ **1.** The police, courts, and corrections facilities are known as
a. capital punishment.
b. rehabilitation.
c. the criminal justice system.
d. community policing.

______ **2.** The authorization from the court needed by police when there is no witness linking the suspect to the crime is known as a(n)
a. arrest warrant.
b. probable cause.
c. arraignment
d. plea bargain.

______ **3.** A plea of guilty or not guilty from the accused occurs during the
a. arraignment.
b. indictment.
c. corrections.
d. plea bargain.

______ **4.** During a trial, the government's side of the case is presented by the
a. defense.
b. corrections.
c. defendant.
d. prosecution.

______ **5.** A reasonable amount of doubt as to a defendant's guilt will cause the jury to vote to
a. arraign.
b. indict.
c. acquit.
d. parole.

______ **6.** Many cases never go to trial because the accused pleads guilty to a lesser charge, which is called a
a. sentence.
b. plea bargain.
c. parole.
d. rehabilitation.

______ **7.** Imprisonment, parole, and capital punishment are part of the system of
a. corrections.
b. prosecution.
c. rehabilitation.
d. deterrence.

______ **8.** The early release of prisoners who show signs of rehabilitation is called
a. deterrence.
b. prosecution.
c. corrections.
d. parole.

POST-READING QUICK CHECK After you have finished reading the section, list the pros and cons of capital punishment. Use the U.S. Constitution as the basis for your arguments.

____

____

____

CHAPTER 16 Guided Reading Strategies 16.3

Citizenship and the Law

READING THE SECTION As you read the section, place a "T" in front of the true statements and an "F" in front of the false statements in the spaces provided. If false, explain why.

______ **1.** In most states, a delinquent is defined as a person under 18 years of age.

____

______ **2.** One reason for juvenile crime is a lack of parental supervision and guidance.

____

______ **3.** Studies show that high-school dropouts who do not have jobs often become delinquents.

____

______ **4.** Drug addicts often turn to crime as a means of supporting their habit.

____

______ **5.** Peer pressure does not play a major role in a juvenile's breaking the law.

____

______ **6.** A juvenile's guilt or innocence often is determined in a court trial.

____

______ **7.** Juveniles have the same rights of due process as adults.

____

______ **8.** When a youth is 18 or older and accused of a felony, he or she is tried as an adult in most states.

____

POST-READING QUICK CHECK After you have finished reading the section, list the various punishments and alternatives for juvenile offenders. Write the pros and cons of these punishments and alternatives. Decide which you think are most likely to bring about positive changes in the life of young offenders.

____

____

____

Name ______________________ Class ______________ Date ______________

CHAPTER 17 Guided Reading Strategies 17.1

The Economic System

READING THE SECTION As you read the section, fill in the blanks with the correct term or terms to complete each statement.

The United States economy, called a(n) ______________________, is one in which the government does not tell people what to produce or buy. In fact, it is a ______________________ where people have the right to buy and sell goods as they choose, and companies are free to compete with each other in order to make money, or ______________________. ______________________, or the lack of a particular resource, can be an effect of competition and may cause the prices of products to rise. Changes in prices are also often the result of the laws of ______________________ and ______________________. However, business owners in the United States may set any prices they like and run their business in any way they see fit because of the principle of ______________________. ______________________, a system in which the means of production are owned by private citizens, encourages investment, innovation and the production of quality goods. Since competition is an essential part of the economy, business practices that limit competition, such as ______________________, are frowned upon.

POST-READING QUICK CHECK After you have finished reading the section, write a story about supply and demand using snow shovels as the product being sold. Imagine that you own a hardware store in Canton, Ohio. Your story should be written about a one-year period and should show how you would price the snow shovels.

____

____

____

____

Name ______________________ Class ______________ Date ______________

CHAPTER 17 Guided Reading Strategies 17.2

The Economic System

READING THE SECTION As you read the section, match each of the following terms with the correct definition and place the letter in front of the matching term in the space provided.

______ **1.** sole proprietorship

______ **2.** partnership

______ **3.** corporation

______ **4.** stock

______ **5.** stockholders

______ **6.** dividends

______ **7.** nonprofit organizations

a. business owned by one individual

b. shares of ownership in a business

c. people who buy shares in a company

d. profits that go to corporate stockholders

e. businesses such as charities and cultural programs

f. business owned by two or more individuals

g. type of business that is recognized as a separate legal entity

POST-READING QUICK CHECK After you have finished reading the section, write the advantages and disadvantages for each type of business organization. Write the advantages in the first space provided (a) and the disadvantages in the second (b).

1. Sole proprietorship

a. ____

b. ____

2. Partnership

a. ____

b. ____

3. Corporation

a. ____

b. ____

Name ______________________ Class ____________ Date ____________

CHAPTER 17 Guided Reading Strategies 17.3

The Economic System

READING THE SECTION As you read the section, fill in the correct information to complete the chart below.

Four Factors of Production	Definition and Example of Each
1.	**a.**
2.	**b.**
3.	**c.**
4.	**d.**

Write the correct term for each definition in the space provided.

5. Money used to pay for land, buildings, or office space owned by someone else

____

6. Worker output ______________________________

7. Person who risks starting a new business hoping to make a profit ______________

8. Helps small businesses compete in the economy ______________________

POST-READING QUICK CHECK After you have read the section, write an idea for a business venture that you would like to start. List expenses that you think would be required to run your business.

____

____

____

____

____

Name ______________________ Class ______________ Date ____________

CHAPTER 18 Guided Reading Strategies 18.1

Goods and Services

READING THE SECTION As you read the section, fill in the blanks by listing the following information.

1. Measures of economic well-being

a. ______________________________

b. ______________________________

c. ______________________________

2. Industrial power sources (in chronological order)

a. ______________________________

b. ______________________________

c. ______________________________

d. ______________________________

3. Kinds of services

a. ______________________________

b. ______________________________

c. ______________________________

POST-READING QUICK CHECK After you have finished reading the section, write the name of the person that fits each description in the space provided.

1. I revolutionized the way automobiles were built and made them affordable to the masses.

Who am I? ______________________________

2. I brought affordable lighting to American homes and electricity to factories.

Who am I? ______________________________

3. I changed the way computers were sold and met consumers' needs at a lower price.

Who am I? ______________________________

Name ______________________ Class ______________ Date ______________

CHAPTER 18 Guided Reading Strategies 18.2

Goods and Services

READING THE SECTION As you read the section, write the letter of the correct definition in the space provided.

_____ **1.** marketing

_____ **2.** mass marketing

_____ **3.** one-price system

_____ **4.** self-service

_____ **5.** standard packaging

_____ **6.** retailers

_____ **7.** wholesalers

_____ **8.** advertising

a. customers select items and help themselves

b. process of selling a good or service in which the sa product, price, promotion, and distribution are use for all consumers in a market

c. goods already wrapped from the manufacturer

d. companies who own large warehouses where good stored

e. the means of informing customers and persuading them to buy certain products

f. process of making goods and services available and convincing customers to buy them

g. stores that sell goods directly to the public

h. prices are stamped or printed as barcodes on produ

POST-READING QUICK CHECK After you have finished reading the section, list the four main types of transportation used to distribute goods. Write the pros and cons of each in the spaces provided.

Types of Transportation Pros (a) and Cons (b)

1. ______________________

a. ______________________

b. ______________________

2. ______________________

a. ______________________

b. ______________________

3. ______________________

a. ______________________

b. ______________________

4. ______________________

a. ______________________

b. ______________________

CHAPTER 18 Guided Reading Strategies 18.3

Goods and Services

READING THE SECTION As you read the section, write a *T* in the space in front of the true statements and an *F* in front of the false statements. If false, explain why.

______ **1.** Companies advertise generic products.

____

______ **2.** The Nutrition Labeling and Education Act of 1990 requires labels to identify fat and fiber content, serving size, and other nutritional information.

____

______ **3.** A debit card looks like a credit-card but operates like a check.

____

______ **4.** Credit cards are issued by stores, including large retail chains.

____

______ **5.** Charge account and credit-card customers who pay their bills regularly establish a good credit rating.

____

______ **6.** Installment plans allow customers to buy and use a product with a down payment and pay in installments on the balance.

____

POST-READING QUICK CHECK After you have finished reading the section, write some attributes that make a person a good shopper.

____

____

____

____

Name ______________________ Class ______________ Date ____________

CHAPTER 19 Guided Reading Strategies 19.1

Personal Finances

READING THE SECTION As you read the section, fill in the blanks with the correct term to complete each statement.

1. A term used for coins and paper money is ______________________.

2. Mints that make coins for general circulation are located in both ______________________ and ______________________.

3. A written and signed order to a bank to take money from a person's account is a ______________________.

4. A(n) ______________________ is used like a check to deduct money from a person's checking account.

5. Similar to charge cards, ______________________ can be used at a variety of stores.

6. Borrowing for a home or vehicle would be examples of ______________________.

7. Borrowing with the intention of paying for the item within a few weeks or months is an example of ______________________.

8. ______________________ is the legal declaration that a person is unable to pay his or her debts.

9. ______________________ are the people or businesses to whom money is owed.

10. The wise use of credit by individuals, families, and businesses helps the ______________________ overall.

POST-READING QUICK CHECK After you have finished reading the section, write a paragraph for a newspaper column on how to avoid bankruptcy and overextending your finances.

____

____

____

____

____

Name ______________________ Class ______________ Date ______________

CHAPTER 19 Guided Reading Strategies 19.2

Personal Finances

READING THE SECTION As you read the section, fill in the missing information to complete the chart on financial institutions.

FINANCIAL INSTITUTION	DESCRIPTION	SPECIALIZATION
1.		
2.		
3.		
4.		

POST-READING QUICK CHECK After you have finished reading the section, answer the following questions in the spaces provided.

1. What is the Federal Reserve System? What are its purposes?

____

____

2. What steps would a business owner take in order to get a bank loan?

____

____

Name ______________________ Class ______________ Date ____________

CHAPTER 19 Guided Reading Strategies 19.3

Personal Finances

READING THE SECTION As you read the section, fill in the blanks with the correct term to complete each sentence.

Most families try to save money for unexpected expenses. There are a number of ways to save money. Putting a regular amount in ______________________ can earn interest for the depositor, and banks generally require a small minimum balance on this type of account. When people put a specific amount of money in a financial institution for a certain time period, they are investing in ______________________. Certificates of debt issued by the government, or ______________________, earn interest from the government when they reach maturity. Stocks are another way to save and can be purchased over the Internet or from a ______________________, a person who is employed by a brokerage house. Brokerage houses are members of a ______________________. Buying stocks involves more ________________ than many other types of savings. Many people buy ______________________ because they are less risky than regular stock purchases. ______________________ are mutual funds that buy short-term bonds. Money can be withdrawn from these funds at any time, but this type of investment is not insured by the ______________________. Saving money is not necessarily investing money. Investing money involves earning interest. When you invest your money it is used for expansion in the ______________________. People want to feel that their money is safe in financial institutions, which is one reason why all banks must receive a ______________________ from the state or federal government to operate.

POST-READING QUICK CHECK After you have finished reading the section, name the agency that the federal government established during the 1930s to regulate the stock exchange and explain its function.

____

____

Name ______________________ Class ______________ Date ______________

CHAPTER 19 Guided Reading Strategies 19.4

Personal Finances

READING THE SECTION As you read the section, match the correct definition with each term by wrtiting the correct letter in the space provided.

______ **1.** insurance	**a.** voluntary insurance to cover unexpected losses
______ **2.** premium	**b.** system of spreading risks over large numbers of people
______ **3.** private insurance	**c.** government insurance program that pays money to the states to pay for medical costs of low-income people
______ **4.** beneficiary	**d.** payments to replace lost wages when a person cannot work due to a partial or total disability
______ **5.** disability income insurance	**e.** person named in the policy to receive the money when the policyholder dies
______ **6.** social insurance	**f.** three-part government insurance program that was set up during the Great Depression
______ **7.** Social Security	**g.** government programs that are meant to protect citizens from future hardships
______ **8.** Medicare	**h.** amount a person pays to an insurance company for protection
______ **9.** Medicaid	**i.** government medical insurance program for Americans over 65

POST-READING QUICK CHECK After you have finished reading the section, answer the following questions in the spaces provided.

1. How do insurance companies cover the losses of policyholders when they only collect low premiums?

____

____

2. How could a major natural disaster cause a problem for insurance companies?

____

____

3. What are the three parts of the Social Security program? How is the program funded?

____

____

CHAPTER 20 Guided Reading Strategies 20.1

Economic Challenges

READING THE SECTION As you read the section, match each term with the correct definition by writing the correct letter in the space provided.

_____ **1.** business cycle
_____ **2.** expansion
_____ **3.** inflation
_____ **4.** costs of production
_____ **5.** peak
_____ **6.** contraction
_____ **7.** recession
_____ **8.** trough
_____ **9.** depression

a. period of economic growth
b. severe contraction of the economy
c. highest point of business cycle
d. lowest point of business cycle
e. period of economic slowdown
f. severe trough, very hard economic times
g. the ups and downs of the economy
h. rise in prices
i. includes wages, transportation, rent, raw materials

POST-READING QUICK CHECK After you have finished reading the section, answer the following questions about the economic changes brought about by the Great Depression.

1. When did the Great Depression occur? Name one cause of the Great Depression.

____

2. What economic theory did the Great Depression seem to discredit?

____

3. What was the name of Franklin Roosevelt's program to deal with the Great Depression?

____

4. Why was the Social Security system created? What does the program provide?

____

____

____

____

Name ______________________ Class ______________ Date ____________

CHAPTER 20 Guided Reading Strategies 20.2

Economic Challenges

READING THE SECTION As you read the section, fill in the correct information to complete the main points concerning the economy.

Most serious challenges to the economy:

1. ____________________

2. ____________________

3. ____________________

Causes of economic challenges and problems:

4. ____________________

5. ____________________

6. ____________________

7. ____________________

8. ____________________

Government responses to economic challenges:

9. ____________________

10. ____________________

11. ____________________

Consumer and worker responses to economic challenges:

12. ____________________

13. ____________________

14. ____________________

POST-READING QUICK CHECK After you have finished reading the section, think about the ways consumers and workers can aid in economic recovery. Then write a plan explaining how you and your family can do your part to help with economic challenges in this country.

____

____

____

____

Name ______________________ Class ______________ Date ______________

CHAPTER 20 Guided Reading Strategies 20.3

Economic Challenges

READING THE SECTION As you read the section, provide the correct term for each description in the space provided.

1. ______________________ organizations formed by workers to obtain higher wages and improve working conditions

2. ______________________ representatives of workers and the employer meet to reach an agreement

3. ______________________ union members walk off the job because their demands have not been met by employers

4. ______________________ striking workers march in front of their workplace to discourage other workers from working

5. ______________________ work slowdowns or other actions short of a strike

6. ______________________ guarantees the right of workers to organize and collectively bargain with employers and set up the NLRB

7. ______________________ allows the president to order workers to delay a strike

8. ______________________ prevents certain abuses by union officials

9. ______________________ a recommendation is made by an expert in a labor dispute

10. ______________________ a binding decision is made by an expert in a labor dispute

11. ______________________ laws that ban the closed shop

12. ______________________ workers must be union members to be hired

13. ______________________ largest association of unions in the United States

POST-READING QUICK CHECK After you have finished reading the section, describe the plight of workers in factories during the 1800s.

____

____

____

____

Name ______________________ Class ______________ Date ______________

CHAPTER 21 Guided Reading Strategies 21.1

The U.S. Economy and the World

READING THE SECTION As you read the section, match each of the following terms with the definition by placing the correct letter in the space provided.

_____ **1.** market economy

_____ **2.** consumer

_____ **3.** producer

_____ **4.** circular-flow model

_____ **5.** demand

_____ **6.** law of demand

_____ **7.** supply

_____ **8.** law of supply

_____ **9.** competition

_____ **10.** stock

a. amount of goods and services people want and will pay for

b. when prices go up and people want less of an item

c. amount of items producers provide at a given price

d. person or company that produces goods and services

e. providing more goods and services when prices go up

f. economic rivalry among businesses selling the same item

g. when the government plays no role in making economic decisions

h. person who buys goods or services

i. represents ownership in a corporation

j. shows the exchange of resources, money payments, and products

POST-READING QUICK CHECK After you have finished reading the section, describe the following: traditional economy, command economy, market economy, and mixed economy.

____

____

____

____

Name ______________________ Class ______________ Date ______________

CHAPTER 21 Guided Reading Strategies 21.2

The U.S. Economy and the World

READING THE SECTION As you read the section, determine which of the multiple-choice items is the correct answer for each statement. Put the letter of the appropriate answer in the space provided.

______ **1.** The ups and downs of the economy over time is called
a. free enterprise. **c.** capitalism.
b. the business cycle. **d.** economic growth.

______ **2.** The highest point in the economic cycle is the
a. trough. **c.** peak.
b. expansion. **d.** contraction.

______ **3.** The lowest point of the economic cycle is the
a. trough. **c.** peak.
b. expansion. **d.** contraction.

______ **4.** When a downturn in the economy is particularly bad, it is called a(n)
a. recovery. **c.** expansion.
b. contraction. **d.** depression.

______ **5.** Business investment can promote economic expansion by
a. buying capital goods. **c.** improving efficiency.
b. investing in research. **d.** all of the above

______ **6.** People and businesses generally borrow more money when
a. they believe the economy is weak. **c.** interest rates are low.
b. oil prices are high. **d.** interest rates are high.

______ **7.** Which of the following is a leading indicator that the government relies on to predict the economic future?
a. building permits **c.** number of new businesses
b. people's incomes **d.** birthrate

______ **8.** Which of the following would give immigrants "permanent resident" status?
a. a visa **c.** a green card
b. a passport **d.** all of the above

______ **9.** Which of the following affects economic growth?
a. the business cycle **c.** neither of the above
b. current events **d.** both of the above

POST-READING QUICK CHECK After you have finished reading the section, write a paragraph on how the perceptions and expectations of people and businesses can affect the economy.

Name ____________________ Class ____________ Date ____________

CHAPTER 21 Guided Reading Strategies 21.3

The U.S. Economy and the World

READING THE SECTION As you read the section, write the word or phrase that matches each statement in the space provided.

1. Protecting workers and consumers, pollution controls, and encouraging competition are examples ____________

2. The Food and Drug Administration helps with this goal ____________

3. Tax reductions for businesses that follow certain policies the government favors ____________

4. In the United States, the Federal Reserve decides this ____________

5. Unemployment compensation is an example ____________

6. When the economy is contracting, and government increases the money supply ____________

7. When government raises the interest rate to slow economic growth ____________

8. The buying and selling of government securities ____________

POST-READING QUICK CHECK After you have finished reading the section, explain how the Fed uses each of the following tools of monetary policy.

Open-market operations ____________________

____

____

Discount rate ____________________

____

____

Reserve requirement ____________________

____

____

Name ______________________ Class ______________ Date ____________

CHAPTER 21 Guided Reading Strategies 21.4

The U.S. Economy and the World

READING THE SECTION As you read the section, complete the following statements by filling in the blanks with the correct term from this section.

Because people and countries ______________________ in producing certain kinds of goods or services, international trade is possible. The reliance that people and countries have on each other is called ______________________. Countries determine what to specialize in by looking at ______________________ and ______________________. This is looking at what products and services the country can produce more cheaply than its trading partners and that offer the most profit for the country. In making these economic decisions, all countries must make ______________________, or economic sacrifices. When a country decides to specialize in one area, the ______________________ is the value of what the country chooses to give up.

Some countries have set up ______________________ that limit the exchange of goods and services. Taxes that are placed on ______________________, or goods coming in from other countries, are called ______________________. Another barrier, ______________________, limits the amount or number of a certain good or service that can be imported. A(n) ______________________ completely bans trade with a particular country. Trade without any restrictions is called ______________________. Some people support policies that give domestic goods an advantage.

The income from other countries versus the amount a country spends with other countries is called a country's ______________________. If a country sells more than it buys, there is a(n) ______________________. If a country buys more than it sells, there is a(n) ______________________.

POST-READING QUICK CHECK After you have finished reading the section, define the terms absolute advantage and comparative advantage in the space provided.

____

____

____

____

Name ______________________ Class ______________ Date ____________

CHAPTER 22 Guided Reading Strategies 22.1

Career Choices

READING THE SECTION As you read the section, decide which statements are true and which are false. Write a *T* in front of the true statements and an *F* in front of the false statements. If false, explain why.

______ **1.** The freedom to choose your own career is never limited by economic conditions.

____

______ **2.** Personal values are not important in determining what occupation to seek.

____

______ **3.** Some people choose jobs because of high pay or the chance to help others.

____

______ **4.** It is important to look at your qualifications before choosing a career.

____

______ **5.** A good education improves the chance of obtaining a high-paying career.

____

______ **6.** Employers typically want workers with special training for each position.

____

______ **7.** Employers look for workers that have a good education, the right skills, and the right attitude.

____

POST-READING QUICK CHECK After you have finished reading the section, make a list of the advantages of having a good education.

____

____

____

____

____

____

CHAPTER 22 Guided Reading Strategies 22.2

Career Choices

READING THE SECTION As you read the section, match each term with the correct definition by writing the correct letter in the space provided.

______ **1.** white-collar workers	**a.** workers whose jobs require manual labor
______ **2.** professionals	**b.** workers such as doctors and lawyers who have many years of education and training
______ **3.** technicians	**c.** people who operate machines or equipment
______ **4.** blue-collar workers	**d.** workers who perform heavy physical work
______ **5.** apprenticeship	**e.** people who perform jobs that require specialized skills
______ **6.** operators	**f.** businesses that sell services, not products
______ **7.** automation	**g.** use of machines instead of workers
______ **8.** laborers	**h.** farms run by large corporations
______ **9.** agribusinesses	**i.** people who work in professional, technical, managerial, sales, or administrative support jobs
______ **10.** service industries	**j.** fixed period of on-the-job training

POST-READING QUICK CHECK After you have finished reading the section, answer the following questions about the different types of occupations discussed.

1. What jobs might a person learn through an apprenticeship?

____

____

2. Why has the number of machine operators in American industry decreased?

____

____

____

3. What are some examples of service industries?

____

____

____

Name ______________________ Class ______________ Date ____________

CHAPTER 22 Guided Reading Strategies 22.3

Career Choices

READING THE SECTION As you read the section, turn each of the headings in the section into questions using the words who, what, why, when, where, or how. Then answer the question in the space provided. See the sample below.

1. Careers in Government

Question: How many Americans work for the federal government?

Answer: more than 2.7 million Americans

2. Federal, State, and Local Government

Question: ____

Answer: ____

3. Armed Forces

Question: ____

Answer: ____

4. Growing Industries

Question: ____

Answer: ____

5. Workers in Demand

Question: ____

Answer: ____

6. Unemployment

Question: ____

Answer: ____

7. Equal employment opportunity

Question: ____

Answer: ____

POST-READING QUICK CHECK After you have finished reading the section, explain what the phrase "equal opportunity employer" means.

Name ______________________ Class ______________ Date ______________

CHAPTER 22 Guided Reading Strategies 22.4

Career Choices

READING THE SECTION As you read the section, fill in the missing information in the spaces provided.

1. Name seven ways to find out more about careers.

a. ______________________ **e.** ______________________

b. ______________________ **f.** ______________________

c. ______________________ **g.** ______________________

d. ______________________

2. Write the seven questions that help evaluate possible careers.

a. ______________________ **e.** ______________________

b. ______________________ **f.** ______________________

c. ______________________ **g.** ______________________

d. ______________________

POST-READING QUICK CHECK After you have finished reading the section, write what you think is the best way to learn about careers and why.

____

____

____

____

____

____

Name ______________________ Class ______________ Date ______________

CHAPTER 22 Guided Reading Strategies 22.5

Career Choices

READING THE SECTION As you read the section, write the term that fits each description. You may check your answers by unscrambling the word or phrase that is provided for each statement.

1. Printed form on which you supply information about yourself.

______________________________ lptpncaioia

2. This tells employers about your grades and the subjects you studied.

______________________________ holcso thisyor

3. A list of these activities tell employers about your potential skills.

______________________________ raxelutrciacurr

4. These might help an employer know and understand you better—for example, by indicating if you are more of a leader or a follower.

______________________________ cipelsa teetnissr

5. How well, fast, and accurately you use your hands is an indication of these.

______________________________ romto lsslik

6. These determine how well you can visualize or picture things in your mind.

______________________________ laurecptpe isklsl

7. These determine how well you work with others and interact with the public.

______________________________ slaortinpeern sliksl

8. These exams help you explore yourself and assist in discovering your abilities.

______________________________ detupati setts

POST-READING QUICK CHECK After reading the section, list different kinds of skills and which jobs might require each.

____

____

____

____

Name ______________________ Class ______________ Date ____________

CHAPTER 23 Guided Reading Strategies 23.1

Foreign Policy

READING THE SECTION As you read the section, fill in the blanks with the missing information to complete each statement.

The plans a country has for its interaction with other countries is called ______________________. Because of advances in communication, trade, and transportation, the countries of the world have become more ______________________. The President of the United States is the chief diplomat and is also the ______________________ of the U.S. armed forces. The president has the power to make treaties with foreign countries with the approval of the ______________________. Sometimes the president and a foreign leader reach a mutual understanding or ______________________ rather than a formal treaty, which would need no further confirmation. The ______________________ is appointed by the president and heads the State Department. This person advises and assists the president and oversees the ______________________, which includes all U.S. ambassadors, ministers, consuls, and their assistants. The cabinet department that informs and advises the president on military matters is the ______________________. The secretary of defense and the president receive military advice and information from the highest officers of the military branches. Collectively these officers are known as the ______________________. Other agencies have been formed by Congress to establish and carry out foreign policy.

The ______________________ gathers information about military and political trends and developments in various countries. The ______________________ was created to help coordinate military and foreign policy. Because of the checks and balances built into the Constitution, Congress also has many powers in U.S. foreign policy.

Congress must approve presidential treaties with a ______________________ vote.

POST-READING QUICK CHECK After you have finished reading the section, write a paragraph on why it is important for the president and Congress to work together on foreign matters. Use the League of Nations as an example.

____

____

Name ______________________ Class ______________ Date ____________

CHAPTER 23 Guided Reading Strategies 23.2

Foreign Policy

READING THE SECTION As you read the section, match each of the following terms with the correct definition and place the number of the right answer in the correspon-ding square in the box below. If the squares all have the correct number placed in them, each of the columns and rows will add up to 21. There are three extra answers.

a. difference in the value of imports and exports
b. meeting between leaders of two or more countries on issues of mutual concern
c. goods and services a country sells to other countries
d. diplomats traveling back and forth between different countries
e. conducting relations between countries
f. goods a country buys from other countries
g. agreement designed to eliminate trade barriers between the United States, Canada, and Mexico
h. government program that provides economic or military assistance to another country
i. when Congress granted more than $13 billion in aid to European countries after World War II

1. shuttle diplomacy
2. European Union
3. environmental diplomacy
4. Marshall Plan
5. exports
6. foreign aid
7. summit
8. diplomacy
9. balance of trade
10. trade deficits
11. NAFTA
12. imports

a.	**b.**	**c.**
d.	**e.**	**f.**
g.	**h.**	**i.**

POST-READING QUICK CHECK After you have finished reading the section, write the full names and give a brief description for each of the following:

1. OAS ____

2. ANZUS ____

3. NATO ____

4. EU ____

5. APEC ____

6. WTO ____

7. IMF ____

Name ______________________ Class ______________ Date ____________

CHAPTER 23 Guided Reading Strategies 23.3

Foreign Policy

READING THE SECTION As you read the section, fill in the blanks with the correct answer for each of the six divisions of the United Nations.

A. General Assembly

1. ______________ number of votes per member

2. ______________ majority needed to pass important issues

B. Security Council

3. ______________ number of members

4. ______________ number of permanent members

5. ______________ number needed to pass measure

6. ______________ number of permanent members needed to defeat a measure

C. International Court of Justice

7. ______________ number of judges

8. ______________ number of years in term

9. ______________ needed for court decisions

D. Economic and Social Council

10. ______________ purpose or mission

11. ______________ areas of study

E. Trusteeship Council

12. ______________ created after this

13. ______________ suspended this year

F. Secretariat

14. ______________ title of person in charge

15. ______________ term of office

POST-READING QUICK CHECK After you have read the section, name the five permanent members of the UN Security Council.

____

____

____

CHAPTER 24 Guided Reading Strategies 24.1

Charting a Course

READING THE SECTION As you read the section, answer the questions in the blanks provided.

1. What three problems hampered President Washington's policy of isolationism?

____

2. What were three causes of the War of 1812? ______________________

____

3. Why did President James Monroe issue the Monroe Doctrine? ______________

____

4. How did President Theodore Roosevelt's corollary policy strengthen the Monroe Doctrine? ____

5. Why did the U.S. policy concerning Latin America become known as dollar diplomacy?

____

6. How did President Franklin Roosevelt's Good Neighbor Policy improve relations with Latin America? ____

____

7. How did U.S. senators indicate their support for isolationism after World War I?

____

8. What event brought about U.S. involvement in World War II?

____

POST-READING QUICK CHECK After you have finished reading the section, describe how the entries of the United States into World War I and World War II were similar.

____

____

____

____

Name ______________________________ Class ______________ Date ____________

CHAPTER 24 Guided Reading Strategies 24.2

Charting a Course

READING THE SECTION As you read the section, determine which of the following statements are true and which are false. Write *T* in front of the true statements and write *F* in front of the false statements.

______ **1.** The ideas behind modern communism favored capitalists throughout the world.

______ **2.** Under a communist economic system, the proletariat would control factories and the government.

______ **3.** The Soviet Union turned Western European countries into satellite nations after World War II.

______ **4.** The ideas behind the Truman Doctrine came to be known as containment.

______ **5.** The United States and Britain kept West Berlin supplied by air during the Berlin blockade.

______ **6.** After World War II, communists led by Mao Zedong took over Japan.

______ **7.** The United States used nuclear weapons in the Korean War.

______ **8.** Because of the Vietnam War, South Vietnam remains free from communism today.

______ **9.** The reform policies of Mikhail Gorbachev helped end the Cold War.

POST-READING QUICK CHECK After you have finished reading the section, explain why and how the United States became involved in the Vietnam conflict.

____

____

____

____

____

____

____

Name ______________________ Class ______________ Date ______________

CHAPTER 24 Guided Reading Strategies 24.3

Charting a Course

READING THE SECTION As you read the section, describe the United States' relationship with each of the following countries or regions after the Cold War.

1. Russia and Eastern Europe ____

____

____

2. Iraq ____

____

____

3. Israel ____

____

____

4. India and Pakistan ____

____

____

POST-READING QUICK CHECK Match the following leaders (past or present) with the countries or groups they represent(ed). You may use some answers more than once.

______ **1.** Nelson Mandela

______ **2.** Yasir Arafat

______ **3.** Saddam Hussein

______ **4.** Yitzhak Rabin

______ **5.** Ariel Sharon

______ **6.** Osama bin Laden

______ **7.** Hamid Karzai

______ **8.** Mahmoud Abbas

a. Iraq

b. Israel

c. Afghanistan

d. Palestinians

e. South Africa

f. al Qaeda